Hard Hit

ann turner

SCHOLASTIC INC.

New York Toronto London Auckland Sydney
Mexico City New Delhi Hong Kong Buenos Aires

Thanks go to many for their help in the writing of this
To my mother and father, now gone,
for... me the gift
To Tracy Mack, my e... who never ta...
To Jane Yolen, who... as a poet's...
To Fr. Gene... unfailing s... in the midst of death
And for the... even... illumin...

13: 978-0-439-92940-0
...-10: 0-439-92940-7

12 11 10 9 8 7 6 3 2 1   7 8 9 10 11 12/0

...rinted in the U.S.A.   40

First Scholastic paperback printing, October 2007

The display type was set in ChiantiBT and Chauncy Decaf Medium.

The text type was set in Bembo.

Book design by Marijka Kostiw

To my two teenagers

—Ben and Charlotte—

who have each taken their own hard hit

and survived with courage and hope.

table of contents

This is the shoe.

This is the shoe my dad wore

the day we dug in the garden.

This is the shoe my dad wore

the day we dug in the garden

and the phone rang.

This is the shoe my dad wore

the day we dug in the garden,

the phone rang,

and he ran so fast his shoe dropped off.

This is the shoe my dad wore

the day we dug in the garden,

the phone rang,

he ran so fast his shoe dropped off,

and he grabbed the phone and said, "You're sure?"

This is the shoe my dad wore

the day we dug in the garden,

the phone rang,

he ran so fast his shoe dropped off,

he grabbed the phone and said, "You're sure?"

and raced to the bathroom to throw up.

This is the shoe that started

the whole thing,

and I am hurling it hard as I can,

hard as a fastball over home plate

into the wall.

wind up

Mark Warren —

tenth grade —

East Street, Westhampton,

Massachusetts, USA,

the star-cluttered universe.

Two parents, aka mom and dad,

one annoying sister,

one golden dog, Sam,

a few friends.

I suck at math, chess,

and patience.

Good at Magic cards,

skateboarding,

and baseball

handglovesmack

hitcracksail

awe.

Last family reunion

cousins threw hot dogs,

shook soda to explosions,

while Uncle Jake

slapped a baseball

in my hand. "Let's see

how the kid can pitch."

Dad grinned near

the open fire, meat

flared and sparked

I wound up, drilled

that sucker so fast Uncle Jake

couldn't touch it.

Dad ran over, jammed

a hamburger in my hand,

Way to go, Marky!

and clicked his camera —

he only captures

the high moments.

That new girl always sits

in the same gray chair

arm curved like a question mark

on her desk, translating —

Yo. I.

Yo tengo. I have.

Yo tengo un corazón.

I have a heart.

The words flow,

dark hair shifts like

a wave against her

cheek, some sweet smell

when she moves —

Diane.

I'm caught

like a deer

in the lamps of her eyes.

"She's the best," Eddie says.

"Did you see her legs

the way she moves her

mouth?" Eddie snaps his

hand against the porch railing.

"Yeah, I saw."

She's mine!

I want to shout but all

I can do is slap Eddie's hand

and wrestle my best friend

to the sidewalk. He grins.

"Guess you noticed."

Conversation, Mom says

is a tennis game —

lob the ball to her court

she hits it back,

don't slam it, Mark

easy does it, over the net.

In the hallways

I match Diane's quick steps,

talk about school, Mr. Twixit,

with the fizzed hair

and the grim repetition

of Algebra II —

I keep the ball in the air all

the way to lunch,

not bad, Mark, not bad.

"We must be crazy!"

Dad calls, cradling the flame

between red hands.

Josie feeds the fire,

Mom stoops gathering

driftwood Sam bounds and drips

and paws us

this is our favorite place

with the shuttered clam shack

plant our feet

in the cold March sand

the beach holds us

the sky curves down

and the sea is green and cold

and wild.

Josie's thirteen

this year

grown-up filled-out

hair, lips, nails spook me

too much, too soon

and bossy with the mouth.

"Mark! Your night on table,

don't forget — *again!*"

wobbles her arms at me

and I chase her up and down

stairs, grab that mouthy girl

who's still the younger one

and don't let go until

Josie hisses *"Give!"*

Dad always told me —

never, ever give up.

I am in the back

yard with Dad

the sun so sudden hot

I'm a cactus with spines.

He drills the ball,

I hurl it back at the brown

glove before his face —

again and again he shouts,

"Come on!"

I pitch

the leather slams at last

against his nose —

he laughs and throws

his lucky purple hat

on new grass.

Why do I have

to hurt you

before you let me stop?

There's the pressure

from the coach that

back-slapping guy

there's the smell of April dirt

under my feet

as I wind and pitch

and wind again.

The sun blares down

with my arm arced back

Are you lookin'?

Am I okay?

I need a rest today

from coach

and glove and hands

wish I were with Diane.

Dad tapped the telescope

set up in our living room

and told me

we're made from stars —

everything inside

bones, arms, legs

even nose

come from deep black space.

Josie's mouth is

big as a galaxy,

but the eyes of Diane

are star-shine

mirrors

of sky.

Take out the garbage,

brush the dog,

put away groceries,

make the bed, finish homework,

practice pitch to Dad,

"Come on, Marky!"

The words are in my mouth,

tongue and lips

push them out,

"No, Dad, not today."

He looks like Sam

left behind in the drive

but I have a life here

apart from you.

Tonight.

Twelve o'clock?

Be ready.

When Eddie drove up

illegal in his parents' Bug —

I jumped in, we stuck on

geezer hats

and wheeled down the road,

lights like strobes

on slick black tar.

I smoked, choked and threw

the butt out the window,

watched red sparks crash

and blaze behind,

saying

I'm here,

I'm free!

See, there's this prayer

thing, Father Gene says ask

for what you need

what you can't do alone,

doesn't that cover

just about everything?

I kneel and pray

for Diane to notice me,

to be the best pitcher

arm winding back

scooping air, gathering speed

sending the ball flying

over home plate

smack

in the strike zone.

Dad is in the tree

pruning suckers

says spring is late

but trees must be

shaped —

his face is Buddha calm

as he scrapes the saw on gray bark.

I stand beneath

breathing in this wordless

time   no chores

no asking just

him and me.

The phone is ringing —

Dad runs to grab it

sags against the wall

Mom's face is like my

beat-up glove

finally he sits to tell us

words tossed out like fly balls

— tumor — cancer — spread —

Josie tears her napkin into shreds

but why?

You were careful

you jogged, ate prunes, never smoked —

Dad grips his coffee cup,

just bad luck, honey

but we're going to fight

this as long as we can.

I got up and ripped the traitor

phone off the wall

so it could never give us

bad news again.

strike one!

strike one!

It's like the game

Statues where you freeze

in position —

Mom's hand is on

her face,

Dad's staring at the wall,

even Sam rests his nose

on Dad's knee —

Josie asks, "What did

the doctor say?"

The statues don't move

I lean against the wall

words stuck in my mouth

afraid to ask

afraid to hear.

I spent three hours

on the Net last night

searching for a cure,

but I can't tell the crap

from the good stuff:

macrobiotic diet,

herbs, chemo, surgery —

some cancers get seeds

of radiation

to kill the tumor.

Mom says pancreatic cancer

is not that kind,

his doctor's working

on his treatment now.

But it's all too slow

someone tell that white

coat guy

it's my *dad*

we're talking about!

"Your night on table!"

I shouted, but Josie

did not answer — not inside,

or outside I went to the

drooping pine behind

the house — not there —

her bedroom stuffed with

Beanie Babies — not there —

I began to sweat,

finally, flashlight in hand,

under the hallway stairs

I held it high

the beam wavered

on the vial of holy water

in her shaking hand

on Josie's lips

wet with tears.

I curl up under the dark

stairs beside Josie.

My throat is still raw

from the bad news

two nights ago.

She whispers, "Why

is he so sick?"

"Remember — Dad said

stardust makes bone and blood,

kidneys, lungs, and heart?

On the day that Dad began

to grow inside his mom

star clay didn't make

the pancreas

the torn apart

part

and that's why

he's so sick."

I douse myself with holy water

and we climb out

to set the table

silently,

place by place —

together.

I think there's some-

thing wrong with my

eyes everything looks

the same — Eddie leaning

against the wall in science class

Diane smiling at me when

I stumble through Spanish

lunchroom full of talk

and flying words

the coach slapping my back

again — don't they know

everything is changed?

That I'll never be the same?

Mom rattles the sales

papers, snaps the car in gear,

we're off to shop —

anything to get out

of the house.

Two-for-one sale:

one slimy ham,

jam another in the cart;

one bag of onion bagels

Josie throws in three;

one lopsided unfit

cantaloupe lift it

easy no dents please

keep to details

don't let your mind

loose — leash

that sucker

and maybe we'll be

all right.

They are starting my dad

on the medicine trail

like the Cherokee

Trail of Tears

where you stumble

and fall along the hard way.

The doctor pours

a fierce, poisonous river

into his body to shrink

the tumor.

All night my dad throws up,

and I jam the pillow over my head.

This is a hell of a way

to make somebody better.

Biked into town

scrabbled out my money

from lawn mowing

and bought the best Discman

I could find,

handed it to Dad before bed —

"Music helps."

He grinned, hugged me

weak this time —

and stuck the headphones on.

"Disc jockey of nausea,"

he joked.

I ran

before he could see

my tears.

I blew off practice

Monday sat in the den

shades down

jamming my hand

on the controller,

slashing the dark raiders,

killing the trolls

crossing the river of fire,

and at the end,

neck crinked eyes

creamed in their sockets

I felt I'd drawn

a ring of fire

around my dad.

In church today

I shrank against the pew

during the prayers for all

the sick and dying.

When the lector read

Dad's name,

it sounded like

a stranger's.

Everyone bowed their

heads but I kept

mine straight up

— no asking

— no bargaining

— just *heal*.

Eddie knows

asks me over for

target practice.

Lie down, elbows in grass

line my eye up

on a row of cans

close as fear —

click the trigger, gun kicks

each one

high —

Sick!

Tumor!

Growing!

Diane wore this glittery

tank top,

swell–mound–firm

tight blue jeans,

mound–jazz–move

this spicy scent when we

sat in Spanish —

flowers–leaves–smoke

I want to put

my hands on her breathe in

her heat her warmth

that ordinary life.

Dad's treatment

sucks out all his flesh

swipes purple under his eyes

the backs of his hands

and arms have lost

a layer of skin —

I hoe the garden dirt

he stoops and dribbles

lettuce seeds,

wavers, almost falls

I reach out

he pushes me away,

"Going to be a good crop,

Marky." I swear

under my breath words

falling into the earth

like Dad's seeds.

I think I've lost five

pounds the coach punched

my arm — "Feed up, Mark,

big game coming —

how're you doing?"

"Doin' fine," I mumbled

but don't hold me to it,

I said inside

because lies

are so much easier

when we're talking about

my dad slipping away.

Mom told me I had

to get out that

worrying about Dad

would not make him

well. Even Uncle Jake

talked to me on his

cell, "Take a break

buddy."

So I called

Diane, managed not

to drop the phone

and we're on — dance

tomorrow at the school

the smell of sweaty socks

bad music but I

don't care.

We're going.

Mom drove Diane

and me to the dance,

tried to smile

as we raced up the stairs,

leaped into the music —

lights flashed

legs moved

like pistons,

arms waved

all the front of her shining

with stars —

I am walking over darkness

I am dancing on water.

So we've got this science

project for Honors

serious data

serious long-term

project I can't even think

past this *Wednesday*

and he wants five weeks?

Eddie says grow beans

with salt solution —

I could be the guy

with the spit-licked pen

in the pocket protector

marking down a life

a death some thing in between —

my mind scatters

like dust

all I can think is

where will my dad be

five weeks from now?

Dad helped stuff

soil and seeds into

peat moss cups

marked no salt,

low or medium

to see which hurts

and what helps.

Two weeks later

curled green elbows

poke up, reach for

the light —

like my dad

sitting on the porch

this morning,

face held to the sun.

Mom said we had to be

careful, no shouting no

fighting while Dad's so

sick. We promised, I

got out of bed on the right

side, ate breakfast

with my right hand,

smiled at my sister,

brushed the dog did not

talk loud near my dad

he looked so gray

no red anger cloud

at *this* table,

until he's better.

We tried to play

catch in the backyard,

the birds noisy in the black

trees, the first May grass

so bright

I prayed its green fire

would pierce his body

and scorch the tumor inside.

He tilted his lucky purple hat,

I threw too slow and he swore,

"Harder, Mark, harder!

I'm not dead yet!"

The birds flew away

with frightened cries,

then I heaved that ball

so hard he grinned at me

before he collapsed

on the grass.

We could not last one

day Josie wore stacked

shoes staggering down the

stairs makeup on for that disgusting

phone boyfriend

I snapped

watch the eye gook watch the

stairs just *Watch*

she shouted, "You're not my

dad!" I almost slapped

but held my hand

man

it felt so great

to be angry

instead of sad.

Today I got my skate

board out of the

closet and put on

blue sneakers, gray sweatshirt,

my Red Sox hat —

and bummed a ride to

town where I laid down

tracks

behind the school

until the wind blinded

me and tar raced

away under my feet,

no end no beginning

just speed and wind.

I hate meals how

he struggles to eat

all day I worried that

he can't get well

on juice and air,

but in Spanish class

looking at the blue sky

of Diane's eyes I pulled

the answer out like a rope

whipped free from a snag —

I'll make my own sacrifice

like in the Bible

something no one's ever done

in high school —

I'll pitch a no-hitter

against Northampton High

for my dad.

At church today the words

were about Lazarus

that old creep stuck

in the tomb falling

apart his nails dropping

off eyeballs slipping

but he walked

out they picked the maggots

off his skin

if *he* can do it

so can Dad

I just wish resurrection

was easier.

Eddie's my doctor

gives me silence

without questions

as we drive up the

bumpy country road

to a place

in the hills.

We walk

to the black lake

throw stones

into glassy water

and noise explodes —

trumpet honks

wings thump,

we race down the road

to the safe car.

"Jesus!" Eddie touches

his saint's medal

but I feel washed

by something so clean

so fierce

it's like a prayer.

"Eddie told me

about your dad."

It's Diane on the phone

breathless,

"I lit a candle for him

and it burned all night.

Grandma says that's

a sign of hope."

I cup the phone,

holding her words,

keeping them safe.

"You've gotta,"

the coach shouts,

pay attention

pitch harder

beat Northampton High —

but my arm's all twisted

eye's a slit

of useless information

the ball goes wild —

he can't see how fear

screws me up.

Eddie knows about

the sacrifice I've got

to make, crouches in my drive,

glove held high —

I lean back, wind up,

hurl the ball again

and again past

the stick Diane holds

to measure the strike

zone in red.

When sweat drips

on my tongue I finally

make two out of three.

Diane asks, "Is that good?"

Eddie shouts

and flings his glove

in the air.

Mom is cooking up a storm

tearing around the kitchen

spoons fly bowls clatter

the mixer whirs

she's a blur of white

and black hair flying —

After the buzzer rings

in the sudden quiet

she sings the names

of food like the litany

of the saints —

"Spaghetti Bolognese,

garlic mashed potatoes,

carrots sweet with brown sugar,

floating island, come eat,

you need to eat!"

He begins to smile,

spoons up meringue

and makes a white circle

round his mouth.

We sit,

dazed with grace.

extra innings

"Good news, good news!"

they are crazy dancing laughing

after Dad's new CAT scan.

Champagne cork pops

fizzy bubbles

prick my nose,

relief sears my throat.

"Treatment's working!"

Dad kicks his heels,

"Working!" Josie slaps his hand.

"Working," Mom chants.

I race to the closet,

yank out his purple hat

and jam it on his head —

luck we got

luck

at last.

Whispering in Spanish

class, "Hey," the word

scatters, "my dad's

better."

"Hey," she touches

my hand,

"remember

the candle burned

all night."

Mi corazón

I remember.

Dad wrestled me

to the rug today,

hugged my head my arms

my shoulders, pressed

me down

breath squashed between

my ribs

but when we stood

sweating and shouting

I almost hit him

I loved him so.

Mom was shy

almost secretive

setting up this altar

on the bookcase with

statues of Mary, St. Michael,

Jesus, photos of Gran,

a bouquet of violets,

and four white candles.

We each lit one

and whispered

thankyouthankyouthankyou

as the smoke rose

to the living room ceiling.

It's that Duke Ellington

stuff the big band

sound Dad swings

Mom round the living room

kicking up his right

foot

she laughs he pulls

her close kisses

her neck

I can hardly stand

to watch

my heart is strange

and full

I don't know if

it's love or fear,

but Josie jumps up

to dance with them

on the red flowers

of the rug.

The big game's

coming close one more

game to get ready to

pitch that no-hitter

here I am

ball cupped in the socket

of my hand heading

for that slot

between chest and knee —

I hope I can do it

EddieDiane tell me I can —

yells erupt,

strike one! strike two!

Again and again,

five long innings

until my arm unwinds

something lets go

batter gets a hit

but from the stands

I hear Dad shout,

"Way to go, Marky!"

It's not good enough — not yet.

Diane is sitting at

our table for the first

time my breath catches

will they like each other?

Dad asks questions, hands out

tea and cookies, suddenly

they switch to Spanish —

I am on the outside

looking in except

Diane looks up,

her eyes blaze

with something so fiery

my breath comes free.

Dad sets his tea down

a satisfied look

on his face.

Uncle Jake is back

with his handlebar moustache

his bad jokes

cigar smoke

on his shirt —

he catches my fastballs

in the backyard

no praise no blame,

sits with Dad and gulps

Millers, thumps the can

down spits out words

about the state of the world —

a door swings wide —

I suck in a deep breath.

I'm back

in normal life again.

We drove to the beach

Dad loves

with the gold sand

and the gray shack

selling clam bellies.

Dad walked to the sea,

stumbling in the late May wind.

Mom wailed,

"Maybe this is not

a good idea."

But Dad lifted his face

to the wind the sun the sea

and the sparkles that lifted off

the green water flew

into his eyes.

He said that seeing

the things you love

is always a good idea.

We make a circle

on the floor

Dad deals out cards

smooth as Vegas

under his purple hat brim,

telling us how to bid

and fake and fold.

I bet way beyond

my hand, throw all my

chips onto the red rose

of the rug —

I bet on

Dad's life.

Practice cancelled,

home early

heard Mom on the phone,

voice choked

with that bad news

sound, "You're sure?"

I yanked on

running shoes,

sprinted up the hill

in the rain,

kicked stones

spit and prayed

to pitch that no-hitter,

no room for failing now.

three strikes!

three strikes!

The prayers, trying

not to fight with Josie

and walking careful

did not work

because, Mom told us,

fingers fidgeting around

her mouth,

Dad's tumor

is growing again.

It never left,

lurked behind

the stomach

took cover

under the liver.

Dad slowly walks the

hallway at night,

and I am wearing out

the palm of my glove.

Josie and I watch

Titanic

three nights running,

leaning forward waves

slam against the deck,

people jump without

hope without life jackets

into the raging sea below.

I grab her hand

imagine jumping

into the wild ocean

saving

each other.

Diane asked me how

I was doing today

words bunched behind

my lips

my hands trembled she

saw I couldn't talk took

off her sweatshirt

pulled it over

my head — all day

I breathed in

the moss smell of her

all day I caught glimpses

of her in the hall —

kept me from falling.

Here's the data:

no salt — pretty good;

low-salt, grew like

crazy high salt

leaves shriveled, dying

I hold one in my hand

that yellow death

gives me a bad luck

feeling reminds me

of what's happening

behind Dad's skin

in the dark where no one

knows.

The big game is here —

the coach is hunched

in the dugout —

my right arm is blessed

prayed over kissed

and now it winds up

pumps the ball past

that chunk hitter

I blast

and strike them out

for six whole

innings —

Eddie yells

the sun stabs my

eye my arm lets fly

coach shouts

and the chunk sends

the ball out of the park —

a wild searing fall

my dreams falling

with it.

Mom's trying so hard

to keep things normal, said

invite Eddie over

to sleep out back the way

you used to

in the shiny blue tent

with the bent poles.

We sat up late, drank Coke

read Magic books

I played my black deck

under starlight shot out

into space

before Dad was born,

before he ever got sick.

Dad's friend, the lawyer

was here today

at our table,

sleeves rolled up,

yellow pad covered

with scratch marks.

Josie looked at me

and we ran outside

to sit under the long

pine branches.

He has no right

to talk about the future

when there might not be

one.

"Hang on.

You'll get through this,

I know. You're stronger

than you think

and we're all here

loving you."

I open my mouth

take Diane's words

on my tongue like

a communion wafer —

my salvation

for now.

So Eddie,

what do you think happens

when someone dies?

Eddie slaps a card on mine,

opens his mouth, sighs —

Dad thinks we're earth forever,

priest says heaven

begins with now,

my gran once said that souls

join the saints before —

(hope the food is good, I joke).

I tap my card

on his, and

somehow comfort flows out

like sun-warmed water.

Nobody tells you

what it's like

there's no road map

for death

how he just got skinnier

and more wasted until

one awful day

they stuck him in the

hospital where everything

is too white and shiny.

I hold his hand and he squeezes mine —

he can still do that

but I am terrified

of the time

when I touch him

and he won't touch me

back.

I leaned close to catch Dad's

whispered words —

"Too damn white — Marky —

need some color."

I ran home, picked some

green lettuce from the

garden and snatched up

Dad's lucky purple

hat.

He held the lettuce

to his nose — couldn't eat —

tugged on the hat,

brim shading his eyes

but we both know

there's no luck

left.

This time

something in the dirt

holds me up,

it's the end of the season

the shouting from the

bleachers keeps

my eyes clear even

though I know the bargain's

done, all healing

gone.

I wind and pitch

and wind again.

No one can get a hit

on me, no flies, no walks —

the umpire cries *Strike*!

All parts of me

work together,

nine innings of perfection

for my dad.

I want his face

to be the way it used

to be

I want his hands rough

and brown from working in

the dirt I want his grin back,

a white seam in his face.

I whisper kneeling

by the bed, "Dad?

I pitched a no-hitter!"

The damnedest thing, he opened

his eyes and said, "Good boy,

Marky, you always were

a good boy!" He coughed once,

I touched his hand

but he was already

on his way.

So here's what happens.

The death machine whacks us

onto the conveyor belt —

people come and ask their

nosy questions,

gray suit guys with

too-combed hair greet us at

the door where Dad

lies in a box

like an imitation human being.

People kneel and cry,

Mom looks wild

and tired —

I stand in the corner

holding Josie's hand

waiting for it all

to be over.

We huddle in a windy

place where the trees

are talking behind us —

I hold my breath at

the sound of blowing noses

and stuttering tears

my chest feels cluttered

and sore.

The priest's words

lift Dad's spirit

to the sky while

Mom's face crumples,

Josie grips me tight,

and Diane and Eddie

stand on my other side.

Their heat, the sun on her

black hair shining

remind me to breathe.

People are being weird

at school hardly talking

to me or if they do

it's about movies, weather

and sports. *Sports!*

I want to howl

but can't say

what is really happening

inside.

I joke about

the school lunch, algebra class

and my teeth hurt

when the words

scrape past.

Here's what sucks

here's the pits

the knife twist

I didn't see coming —

running to get away

to be free

at the same time

Dad was slipping away.

Now I'm standing alone

now I'm free

and I would cut off

my pitching arm to have him

nag me just once about

the dog the chores the game.

In the middle of

the night when the dark

was an angry mouth

steps pattered down

the hall and Josie

jumped onto the foot

of my bed, pulling

the quilt over her head.

Sam climbed up after,

his nose on my knee.

Josie didn't say a word

just blind animal

warm breathing

helped us sleep

at last.

Mom made a picnic

last night

(Dad used to cook the dogs),

trying so hard with the root

beer floats, hot dogs, homemade

cookies

(Dad would feed the fire)

even a grace she read

as the wind fluttered

her curly hair.

Josie blew her nose,

bit deep, but I

fed my food to the dog.

(Marky, don't turn him

into a beggar!)

There's this smell

I miss

of Dad —

donuts, coffee, suntan

lotion, and sweat.

I ran around and grabbed

his black shirt

purple hat

that damn shoe

and held them in my arms

inside the closet,

sitting there

nose stuffed

with his smell.

Diane and I took the ball

out to the graveyard

where we put Dad

where he's gone

into the earth the air

the fingers of sky

he is sailing dreaming talking

taking holy pictures

We scrape away the dirt

and bury the ball from my

no-hitter

mixing it with his dust —

iloveyouiloveyouiloveyou

Dad.

This time it's

the three of us

Eddie Diane and me

rumbling in the Bug

up the rutted road to

the lake.

We build a fire

roast dogs, drink Coke

throw stones into the

black water — when

the ripples stop

the quiet is like a hand

on my head.

Our breathing floats out

over the water

just us together

in the summer air.

Always hold your glove

in front of your face.

It's irreplaceable.

Don't talk back

to bullies. Use your fist

if you have to.

Remember to kiss

your mom.

She gets lonely too.

Do what you love,

bucks don't count. Remember:

you are lucky and a hundred

million others don't have coats

beds food or clean water.

Hold your hand out

to help.

Love will come

in time.

Never draw to an

inside straight.

Don't forget

to brush the dog.

Lying on my back

looking up

the stars were eyes

blinking in the darkness

hundreds of angels

overhead or all

the dead relatives'

saints

looking down on me.

One star gleamed

and sparked

like Dad's eyes

it seemed he was there

loving me

his dust his bones his voice

part of a star.

national help lines

THE DOUGY CENTER:

THE NATIONAL CENTER FOR GRIEVING CHILDREN AND FAMILIES

1-866-775-5683 (toll free)

www.dougy.org

> The Dougy Center offers peer support groups for grieving children, teens, young adults and their families plus an online directory of grief support programs for children located across the country and internationally.

AMERICAN CANCER SOCIETY

1-800-ACS-2345 (1-800-227-2345) (toll free)

or 1-866-228-4327 for TTY

http://www.cancer.org

> The American Cancer Society is the nationwide community-based voluntary health organization

dedicated to eliminating cancer as a major health problem by preventing cancer, saving lives, and diminishing suffering from cancer, through research, education, advocacy, and service.

Comfort Zone Camp®

1-866-488-5679 (toll free)

www.ComfortZoneCamp.org

The nation's largest bereavement camp for children ages 7–17 who have experienced the loss of a parent, sibling or primary caregiver, camps are held in Richmond, Virginia, and the New York Metropolitan area. The camps are FREE and travel scholarships are available.